The Tao of Design and User Experience

The Best Experience is No Experience

By Andrew Ou

ISBN-13: 978-1542784801

ISBN-10: 1542784808

Get exclusive UX design training from the author and more:

Visit **TaoDesignUX.com**

Version 1.5

Acknowledgements

Mom
Cynthia Or
Reid Christensen
Paulina Lai
Olga Draskovic
Tatiana Malysheva
Susy Hsi
Elle Tsao
Jordon Lui
Jon Chan
Mark Baxter
Nick Lok
Michael Lok
Sarah Hawk
Nikunj Patel
Julian Leonard
Priscilla Lee
Edward Arteaga
Ben Wu

Aurora Winter
Sven Winter
Cassandra Wilson
Robert Matuszak
Tim Forner
Justene Doan
Janice Doan
Wafaa Zain
D'Arcy Henneberry
Zander Sprague
Ann Raisch
Isolde Leung

Edited By:

Andrew Wetmore
Edward Arteaga

Cover Illustration:

Chuqing Zhu

Unlimited Wisdom From:

Bruce Lee

The Story Behind This Book: From the Author

My education and experience have given me a solid understanding of design. But I felt incomplete. I was dissatisfied because, while I understood design fairly well, there were many questions that I still could not answer. And as I observe and listen to other designers, it seems that many, even the most experienced, lack a clear direction. How does one know what one does not know? How could I design a "great experience" if I did not know what the "best" was? What defines "great"? What is the true definition of "simple"? These were the most basic questions, yet no one could produce a definition I was satisfied with. Many designers want to design for a "great" user experience, but even "great" lacked definition. When the foundation is weak, the branches cannot be strong.

I set out to find the truth, to discover myself, and to find my way. Answers from different sources varied from practitioner to practitioner, and many of them lacked the clarity I was seeking.

Answers to "great experience" ranged from "elegant UI" through "pleasurable" and "functional" to "delightful", and all their variations. While some of them were valid answers, they lacked the depth I was looking for. No truths could be found within the design realm.

In order to understand design from a new perspective, I had to look beyond the field of design, at a level higher than design itself. I turned to martial arts and philosophy, and drew from the infinite wisdom of Tao, and *The Tao of Jeet Kune Do* by Bruce Lee, combined with my knowledge as a martial artist. With that, I was able to create an intersection between design and martial arts, to draw a new form, a new way of thinking, ultimately paving the way I practice design.

I can confidently state that the deepest things I've learned about design did not come from design itself. Rather, they came from my understanding of martial arts. The philosophies are infinitely deeper than design itself, which is why it is highly capable of cultivating design thinking beyond design.

I have not invented a new style, process, or convention to design. *The Tao of Design and* User *Experience* is a philosophy of guiding thoughts which leads to the truth beyond all complexities. I hope to free my followers from fixed patterns, conventions, or "standards" which are then taken as the gospel, and then become a tradition too rigid to evolve. My approach is direct and simple. It does not contain artificial definitions, fixed forms, or anything that is inessential. The key to extraordinary design is simplicity. To master design, you must first master yourself. This unique intersection would not have easily come from anywhere else, which is why I wanted to express it to the world.

How to use this book

The principles here are to strengthen you, at the root, as the practitioner of the art of design, more specifically, UI / UX design. Do not patch the leaves and branches, when it is the roots and the trunk of your art that require proper direction to grow.

This book is meant to help remove you from limitations so you can see the truth, and to bring fluidity to your mindset and way of thinking so you can discover a way that is *your* way.

Approach the philosophies and ideas here with a blank slate. Set aside all your current knowledge about design. Reintroduce abstraction and fluidity to your mindset to broaden your way of thinking, so you can merge these principles with your own understanding of design, and arrive at a new, advanced practice of design. Interpret the concepts in your own way, and apply them as you see fit.

While the illustrations of these principles relate specifically to UI / UX applications, the philosophies are much higher and deeper than design itself. They are bound to no form and are unlimited in their applications. Thus, they possess the fluidity to manifest themselves beyond the user interface of an application, in multiple forms of art, and even in life itself.

Time displaces knowledge, so having knowledge is not enough. Knowledge is a point in time, whereas knowing is a trajectory. The philosophies here focus on discovering your trajectory, so you can acquire the freedom to advance. They'll nurture you, the practitioner, as the root of all your creations, so that you can seek and express the truth yourself.

Design encompasses both art and science. Art considers unlimited possibilities, but science grounds them in reality. While this book focuses on the art aspect, **never forget the science of testing and data in practice**. The art may evolve without limitations as long as we do not violate the fundamentals.

You will achieve advanced mastery of the art of design and user experience by understanding that, ultimately, the best experience is to have no experience. But first you must solidify your grasp of the fundamentals of design, so you are strong on all fronts. Then you can open your mind to new ways of thinking. You will not be able to fully appreciate advanced concepts without a solid foundation, nor will you be enlightened with a closed mind.

The principles here are meant to liberate you, not to bind you to a certain form.

You. The creator. The seed.

Enrich the seed. Enrich the blossoming.

3

If we establish a genuine doctrine, it forms a trajectory that abides indefinitely.

Philosophy

Philosophy is the fundamental nature of knowledge. It is the foundation for everything. It is what guides us as we venture through the unknown. It allows us to know the unknown, and find a way of knowing within it. Philosophy is the seed that guides all the branches into their proper form.

Without a philosophical reasoning, our movements and our actions are without intent. We don't know the how, the what and why of what we do. It is through philosophy that we find richness in our reasoning, and meanings in our actions.

Philosophy is the root where everything begins, so if we establish a genuine doctrine, it forms a trajectory that abides indefinitely.

Tao

To achieve enlightenment and the state of knowing, one must eliminate reliance on existing methodologies, processes, ideas or "knowledge". Time and evolution disrupt knowledge and ideologies, so obtaining knowledge is not enough. Rather than seeking knowledge, seek the enlightenment that allows for unbounded understanding and expansion into the known and the unknown.

Design is ultimately a form of art. When you understand it as art, you understand that it is devoid of limitations.

Pursue that which will allow the definition of truths from your own expression as a practitioner of the art: the art of design and user experience.

The art of design and user experience is a methodology, an idea, a process, which can only exist through a living soul, a living practitioner. The art ceases to exist without a living practitioner, and ceases to evolve if we practitioners do not dynamically give it a new meaning. The art does not give itself new meaning, but we can. Thus, the living practitioner, the human being, is more important than any one methodology, idea, or process.

Knowledge, and definitions of what we know, exist as a form. Do not cling to forms. We can always break forms down and infuse them with new meaning. Forms do not evolve themselves. Forms only evolve through a living example.

As human beings, we all express ourselves uniquely. Our craft is the element of our creativity and expression, externalized into tangible, physical existence.

Understanding the principles of design is not enough. Understanding yourself as a designer, and as a human being, fosters limitless methods of knowing the unknown, and this knowing will always lead you toward the truth.

The execution of creativity originates from a human being as the creator. Instead of focusing on the branches of creation, focus on the creator, the seed itself.

Knowledge is only a point in time, but knowing is a continuous movement.

To be knowing is to be able to devise new knowledge in the void. It is to be able to create light in darkness, and to know the unknown without external sources.

Without a founding philosophy, and a proper guiding principle, your work ceases to evolve with intention. It becomes merely a set of meaningless mechanical movements.

Use no way as a way.
To have no form is to be able to assume all forms.

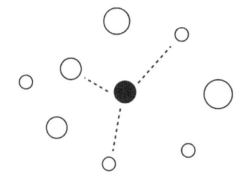

Knowledge

Knowledge will only foster your level up to a certain point. It only exists as a certain point in time.

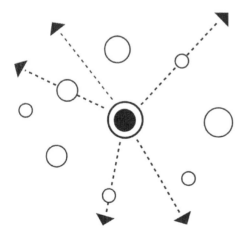

Knowing

But knowledge on self, and way of knowing will allow you to discover your rhythm, and create a trajectory, a way, when there is no way. It has no limitations.

The Tao of User Experience is a principle of action without action, a principle of effortless doing:

No interface as interface

No interaction as interaction

No experience as experience

Without experience, users can achieve goals without achieving goals

To have no experience is to have every experience

The Fundamentals

What is Design?

This is a simple question, yet the answers are complicated. The answer varies from designer to designer, and the nature of the answer is often intertwined with the practitioner's specific design domain. For a graphic designer, "design" may be related to "visuals". For an architect, the definition may revolve around "form" or "function". Many others perceive design as how an object or interface looks, mainly because for them the design exists through a presentation layer: the presentation is the most important and apparent part of the design. Others may speak of function, or anything else in between.

The answers are misleading and ornamented, because they only encapsulate a partial understanding, even when it is an experienced practitioner who provides the answer. The answer should be simple, yet few can offer a true, satisfying definition of design.

Foundation is key because everything stems from it. Never forget that, regardless of how experienced you are as a designer. If you cannot craft a simple and solid definition of design, you will not be able to grasp the essence of design at higher levels. However, if you strengthen your foundation, it will enrich all the branches of design that you practice and help you articulate a clear and powerful definition. Thus, it is crucial to understand "design" in its truest form before understanding its branches.

Whether you practice graphic design, industrial design, fashion design, UI / UX, or something else related to design, you must understand design in its most fluid form. When designers practice a certain branch of design, they eventually, unintentionally adopt a branch-specific definition of design, one that is crystallized and localized to their domain of practice. This partiality of understanding shadows many from understanding "design" in totality.

Understanding "design" in totality allows for boundless expansion. Begin by eliminating all the fragments and branches of what you know about "design", and start with an empty slate. When you see "design" in totality, it is void of all obscurity, fragments, and pieces of incomplete contamination that prevent you from achieving enlightenment.

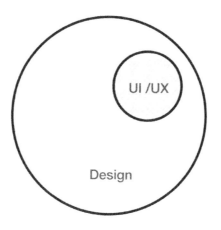

Design in partiality

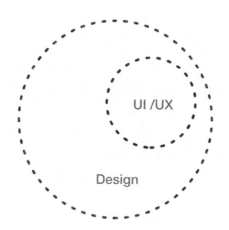

Seek to understand design in totality

When you understand design in totality, you will be able to push design beyond its boundaries and exceed your limitations. Understanding it in totality will also enrich the branch of design you practice.

In the truest form,

To design is to:

Create an entity for a purpose.
To communicate.
To solve a problem.

Note that this definition is void of any relation to a particular department or domain, thus, it is void of crystallization. It is a formless definition of "design" that begins as the root, and it is this fluidity that allows the assumption of all forms, a fluidity that may unite with all the different branches of design.

A design can exist in many forms:

The cup was designed to hold water.

The pencil was designed to externalize thoughts.

The poster was designed to communicate a message.

Design can even exist in a non-physical form. We can design rules, processes and methodologies to achieve certain results. Nature designed our hands to grip everyday objects. As you see, design can be quite abstract, so why limit our understanding of design to a certain branch, or a certain form?

What is an Interface?

An interface, or a user interface, is not simply what it looks like, or what it invites us to do. Interfaces can be abstract, thus an interface is simply a meeting point between two entities:

The handle on the cup allows me (an entity) to hold the cup (another entity).

The pencil allows me to translate my ideas into writing.

The poster is the bridge between me and the message.

The pencil bridges my thoughts, and externalizes them. The arrangement of carefully selected words on a poster is a meeting point which allows me to understand a specific message.

This book is an interface between you and me.

What is Interaction?

We interact with entities every day. Again, an interaction can be abstract as well.

I interact with the cup by picking it up. It is an interface between me and the tea.

I write with the pencil so I can externalize my thoughts on paper.

I read the poster so I can understand the message.

I interact with an idea through thinking.

Thus, an interaction means to act on or with another entity.

As you can see, design can be abstract. Even interfaces and interactions can be abstract. The purpose of the abstraction is to remove limitations, so that it allows for an unlimited means to explore design beyond what we typically observe as an interface, or interaction.

What is Experience? What is User Experience?

Experience is the result of interactions with other entities.

A man goes to the store to buy a product. In order to buy a product, the man must interact with the cashier. The man achieves his goal by receiving the product, and also retains an experience of the entire process. The man can have a positive experience, a neutral experience, or a negative experience, and *that* is experience.

Notice that, in this example, the man interacts with the cashier. Both the cashier and the store are the interface, a meeting point between the man and the product. The experience is the sum of all of the interactions the man makes there. This is known as "Customer Experience". In the technological field, the result of all the user interactions may be identified as "User Experience".

Regardless of the differences, whether it is "Customer Experience" or "User Experience", what remains significant is "Experience".

The definition of user experience

User experience is how a person feels when interacting with the world. The world is comprised of systems, such as computers, doors, humans, and even processes. So user experience is how a person feels when interacting with a computer, a door, a human or a process. User experience is not one specific profession, but, rather, a concept. When we apply this concept to a profession such as interface design, it enhances the design, providing a direction, a reasoning, and a foundation for reasoning.

Mastery of the basics, and having a meticulous understanding of the fundamental definitions of design, interface, interaction, experience, are what separate the novice designer from an experienced one.

It is not possible to be an excellent interface designer, interaction designer, or user experience designer without mastering the basics. It is like mending the branches when the tree cannot stand. The designs cannot achieve a level of depth without a solid foundation of understanding and reasoning.

To understand what constitutes a good experience, or a good interface, one must first understand what experience is, and what interface is. Great solutions to great problems begin with understanding the problem, which will always lead back to the fundamentals.

Principles

The principles I introduce here are not specific to "design". Rather, they are principles focused on enriching your roots, as a designer and as a human being. Knowledge comes from a source. It is a point in time. It may be subject to change and displacement. However, being *knowing* allows you to devise new knowledge when there is no current knowledge.

These are principles of guiding thoughts that exist at a limitless level designed to cultivate, not a wealth of knowledge, but rather, a way of knowing.

Formlessness is to have no form. To have no form is to be able to assume all forms.

Formlessness

Formlessness is the ability to assume all forms. It is bound to no single form, so it can assume all forms. It can be applied to every aspect, from the creator's way of thinking to the creation itself.

Formlessness asserts that the cup can be both half full and half empty, with the fluidity to shift between both ways of thinking. There is no "this" way or "that" way; rather, each way can be truthful in its own way.

There is no "better" or "worse"; rather "different".

The agile mind shifts from criticism to admiration.

Understanding the "wrong" way may also be "right".

Accept that nothing is fixed. Embracing and using uncertainty as an advantage allows you to flow and adapt from moment to moment.

How to Apply Formlessness in Practice

Forms, styles, and methods are subject to limitations. Formlessness clings to no form, so that it can assume all forms. Thus, its only limitation is to have no limitation.

The designer who is formless absorbs and appreciates all the different approaches and essences of creation, and obtains the fluidity to evolve quickly, delivering unorthodox solutions that open the door to great discoveries.

Engage unfamiliarity completely without judgment. Observe with pure objectivity. See what is.

If you meet unfamiliar technology or tools, be ready to adapt to them.

The knowledge you possess as a designer should be constantly changing and evolving.

Do not be quick to reject unfamiliar approaches. Instead, absorb what is useful in it.

If you possess knowledge or principles from other sources and disciplines unrelated to design, you may adapt them to design.

Absorb as much as you can from a variety of people, cultures, and design approaches from around the world. The more you are able to absorb from your encounters and experiences, the more resources you gather to nurture not only your creativity, but yourself as a human being. You will be able to draw from your vast experiences when practicing design.

Formlessness in Mobile App Design

When designing for multiple platforms in mobile applications, there is often a notion that designs must be done an "Android" way or an "iOS" way. When we attach ourselves to this way of thinking, we problematically classify the user as an "Android", or an "iOS" user. We limit our design, our approach, and our understanding by assuming that we must solve the problems we encounter in a certain way. We understand our users as Android, or iOS users, rather than understanding them as **human beings**.

If we can shift our thinking away from such concepts of classification, we liberate ourselves from the limitations imposed by such classifications, providing us with freedom and efficiency in our solutions. Furthermore, we understand our solutions and designs from a human perspective, and that we are ultimately designing for a human being. True design seeks directness.

If we hold a phone with one hand, we are likely to use our thumbs to interact, and are more comfortable with the bottom quadrant of the screen than with the top. Hence, it would be advantageous to place frequent actions, like navigation, at the bottom. If we place navigation at the top, we can supplement it with a secondary form of navigation, such as swiping, for better accessibility. Content should occupy the majority of space without interruption. Buttons should be finger sized, and placed within easy reach. Text should be legible.

Note that, so far, we are making no reference to any particular iOS or Android convention. Rather, the approach to design stems from a bottom-up perspective, aimed at a palm-sized interface for a human being.

If we understand and approach design from this perspective, we are designing for the human way of interaction, rather than being obstructed by the need to satisfy certain styles.

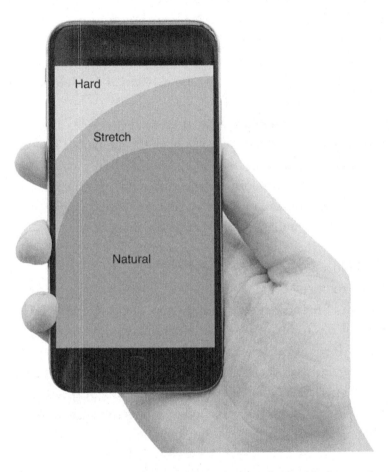

Regardless of whether it is an iPhone or an Android phone, the touch screen phone was designed to be gripped with one hand. Whether we are an iPhone user or an Android user, this is the most dominant way for a user to hold a phone while using the thumb. The natural region is the region where the thumb is most capable of reaching without strenuous effort.

Android and iOS Approach

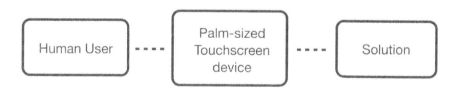

The Human Approach

Facebook mobile UI (Dec 2016)

iOS   Android

One of the most striking differences between Android and iOS is
that iOS utilizes a bottom navigation, while Android utilizes a top
navigation, often supplemented with swipe to navigate.

WeChat mobile UI (Dec 2016)

836 million users Q3 2016

iOS   Android

Wechat, however uses bottom navigation for both iOS and Android, with minor differences. Subsequent interfaces reveal little differences.

https://www.statista.com/statistics/255778/number-of-active-wechat-messenger-accounts/

WeChat Contacts Page

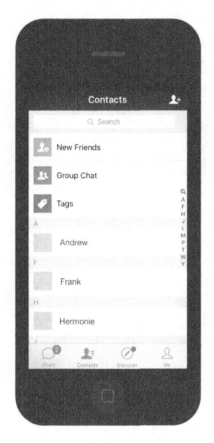

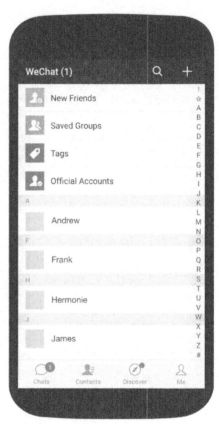

iOS   Android

WeChat Conversation Page

iOS   Android

Which is the correct approach? Can WeChat users all be wrong? After all, there are hundreds of millions of them.

The simple answer is: Both ways are right, and neither is invalid.

While Facebook uses top navigation for Android, and bottom for iOS, it offers clear familiarity to users of both platforms. The approach favours familiarity to the separate users, and conformity with platform conventions.

WeChat, however, uses one design for both. Using one interface for both platforms strongly favours efficiency, with a negligible impact on familiarity. There is minimal need to spend time creating and maintaining a completely different set of designs for each platform.

Websites do not distinguish between Android and iOS. A website does not choose. It simply is: it is an interface for a user with a smartphone.

We were taught conventions. We weren't born knowing them. There are no right or wrongs, no necessary choice between this or that. If the style fulfills its purpose, then that's all that matters.

Formlessness in Styles

May 11, 2016 "Gradients are back"

Skeuomorphism – The design concept in which digital interfaces mimic real world counterparts (left).

The design world experienced a shock when Instagram revealed its shiny new logo, with a gradient of pink, orange and blue. Having moved out of drop-shadows and gradients into the minimalist, flat paradigm, the industry was in need of the Instagram shock. Here was the "new" trend that millions of users and thousands of eager followers had been waiting for, and it was actually no more than a return to gradients.

What makes gradients the new "truth"? And what makes flat design the old? Is it because a major influencer practiced it, or is it the truth because you yourself wholly agree with it?

Though *Instagram* decided to bring back gradients in a new form, it does not invalidate flat design, nor does it revalidate ornamentation.

Skeuomorphism has its strengths and weaknesses. In the early days, ornamentation was necessary to bridging users to digital interface by using real world representations. The skeuomorphic paradigm is now no longer necessary for those who grew up in

Arduino is the Skeuomorphism of IoT

How do we apply this idea to the IoT?

35

the era of digital interfaces. It may however still be applicable for an older generation.

Flat design also has its strengths and weaknesses. While we can appreciate its ideology to strip away ornamentation, the extreme end of minimalism can present usability problems if too many visual cues and information are eliminated. Flat design is a modern choice of design for designers.

All styles have their strengths and weaknesses, thus no style is the best style. Formlessness is to have no form, so you can assume all forms. You are to successfully combine the strengths and discard the weaknesses, shift between them, and apply them as you see fit.

Remember that when you cling too closely to a particular method or style, you will be limited by the rules and laws of that method or style. Your potential and understanding do not escape the shadows of its limitations. A linear and single paradigm of thinking becomes a limitation. However, if you are formless, you obtain the fluidity to adapt and shift between different styles, and can use whichever methods you see fit. There is no 'this' way or 'that' way; rather, each way, and each unique expression, may be correct in its own way.

To express yourself is to learn, but also to forget; to absorb, but also to reject. It is to be in a state of formlessness, yet expressing yourself with the assumption of all forms. It is arriving at a truth, but also being willing to depart from it.

Expression

The Importance of Art in Design

Art is expression. The essence of art is that it favours all possibilities. When you instill art in design, this means that any form, process, practice or solution, no matter how unconventional, can be valid as long as it works.

We, the practitioners, bring design into existence through our creations. Our creations are ultimately the footprints of our expression. We may express forms which have been established, or we can express new forms and ideas which haven't been thought of before. When we do, we begin to give design a new meaning. It is here where design begins to evolve.

Art in design is important because without expression, design becomes a static field which does not evolve. Designers who do not understand the significance of art follow only traditional or "established" patterns, and simply accept what is. They practice according to a set of mechanical patterns, becoming fixated by and bound to the path paved by those who learned to express themselves.

As a designer, you must learn to express yourself truly, and not be subject to limitations, patterns, standards, conventions, or methodologies set by others, the industry, experts, or even the masters.

How to Express Yourself

Expressing yourself truly is to acquire your version of the truth, whether it follows or defies tradition, as long it is your truth. It means acquiring liberty, so you can obtain the fluidity to derive a way that is your own way, one without imposed limitations or forms and that is true to your own expression.

It means expressing yourself, not conventions or received wisdom, at all times. Developing self-expression lets you see with full clarity, without the limitation and subjectivity of established truths.

When you develop a strong ability to rationalize your practice, it creates your rhythm and strengthens your confidence in execution and delivery. The best designers understand themselves deeply, and are highly capable of facing all uncertainties. They devise a complete system, grounded in solid guiding principles. When you establish your foundation it will help you develop an understanding of self and strengthen your approach so that you may thrive even in unfamiliar territories.

Reflect on a "truth", but determine its validity based on your own way of thinking. Do not embrace any observed truth, or "the truth as we know it", unless you, yourself, wholly agree with it.

Expression in UI Design - an example

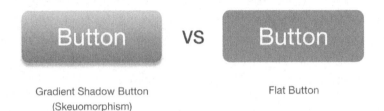

Gradient Shadow Button
(Skeuomorphism)

Flat Button

The skeuomorphic button styles ornamented with shadows and gradients have ruled for at least a decade. Many designers have created buttons like these, many times, over many years, without a significant divergence in style. However, if we use established forms and modes without questioning why a certain style is the way it is, our expression is no more than shadowed tradition. You may understand the tradition and the method, but you do not understand yourself.

There are only two ways to arrive at the truth, one with only your own expression, and one without it.

Flat design is a minimalistic style of interface design that succeeds the outdated skeuomorphic design. It is a choice of many because of its trendy, clean-yet-bold display. It is a dominant choice adopted by designers practicing design in the modern age. Though there are deep reasons that can help explain the rise of flat design, the average designer's understanding only seems to scratch the surface.

Common reasons:

It's the trend
It's clean
It looks simple

While these reasons are valid and quite common, they lack substance and depth. It is easy to copy this particular pattern, but without understanding of the embedded foundations which resulted in this transformation, we only understand its surface, not its implications. We can only replicate this particular style, to the limits of what we observe.

A "trend" is a result of a patternized repetition. The terms "clean" and "simple" are abstract without concrete definitions. If we understand flat design by its cover, we only understand it in partiality, and our knowledge does not extend beyond it. But if we understand it from its roots, we understand it in totality. It is through the acquisition of the depths that we are able to draw the essence from this design trend and even apply it to design beyond the interface.

Flat design - underlying implications:

Because there needs to be no more than it needs to be.

It needs nothing more or less.

Everything that exists, exists for a reason.

There is no ornamentation, no unnecessary decoration, nothing that is inessential.

Most important, it is the simplest form of button that could exist (besides the absence of a button). Can you think of anything simpler?

While it is possible to arrive at the same conclusions that favour flat design, you can do it with a much deeper, comprehensive reasoning. This reasoning is the foundation, and the depth of this foundation allows for application of the design even beyond the interface design.

If you choose to follow a particular style, it is crucial for you to discover yourself, and acquire your own understanding of your choice as the truth, so that, as a result, **it is your expression which merges onto the style, not the style which merges onto your expression.**

While there is no doubt that flat design or its variations are a highly favourable style of the modern era, remember that styles have their limitations. **You must practice formlessness in order to absorb the truth while rejecting the flaws, and have the courage to advance beyond it, or depart from it.**

Identifying and Exceeding Limitations

Forms provide guidance and structure, but when we reach the limits of a form, the form becomes a limitation. We must identify limitations so that, when necessary, we may advance beyond them.

If you follow a trend or pattern, your practice will only be as good as the trend or pattern.

If you only learn from the teacher, you will only be as good as the teacher.

If you cling to practicing design by following conventions, you will be following the steps of those who create conventions.

If you follow a certain process or method, you are subject to the limits of that method.

Conventional solutions are the products of unchanging thoughts, which lead to nothing more than a reinforcement of the current paradigm. It is only when we meet a problem with an unconventional approach that the new approach begins to displace the current way of thinking.

Remember that there is no truth beyond these limitations, so you must create one for yourself.

If you introduce a new form, do not be concerned that it may be unorthodox, as it likely will be. Expect that the unfamiliar will initially meet resistance. It is subject to judgment based on existing knowledge, not the new, internal knowledge that you possess, and it is this limitation of knowledge from others that is responsible for the disconnected understanding of your new form. At first no one, other than yourself, understands your idea completely. However, without new ideas, and unconventional thoughts, there can be no advancement and evolution.

When you introduce a new form or a new idea, you must understand that ideas are abstract and subject to misinterpretation. Ideas only hold potential, but no power on their own. Ideas do not express themselves, nor do they materialize themselves. A living human must manifest the idea to bring it to reality. It is ultimately your will that expresses, and your ability that executes, the idea to its ultimate potential.

An idea can only be as good as the living human being who realizes it.

The Results

When you practice expression, and arrive at a complete level of self-understanding, the distinctions will be clear. You will be able to express yourself and your understanding of the world in the way you specifically practice design, and assert it with confidence. Novice designers follow structure, while advanced designers define it.

Q: Who in the industry do you follow and read?

Novice: I follow _____ because...

Advanced: I like to absorb from _____ and _____, but I
             add what is uniquely my own.

If we follow too closely, we can lose sight of our own expressions and resort to simply copying conventions and solutions set by the leaders. Our expressions will lack depth, bounded by limitations set by others.

However, this does not necessarily mean you should force divergence at all times. It is fair to follow, or copy, if your personal expression aligns with what you are following, so long as you arrive at the truth yourself.

Q: What is the UX design process?

Novice: The UX design process is [textbook definition]

Advanced: The process I work with is [personal definition]

Q: What is the definition of user experience?

Novice: The definition of user experience is [textbook definition]

Advanced: The definition of user experience is [textbook definition], but my definition of it is [insert personal definition]

You may also directly assert your personal definition.

Q: How do you stay on top of current trends?

Novice: I look at [example] to stay on top of...

Advanced: While [examples] are the current trend, I understand that trends may be temporary, and I prefer to follow them as I see fit.

You are not bound by limitations when answering, or when practicing design in a certain way. If you introduce a new form, a new expression, and a new methodology to the world, it can be valid as long as you, the practitioner, can demonstrate it to its fullest potential.

The art of design does not live through a set of established rules. It lives through the practitioner, evolves through the practitioner, and is pushed to new boundaries by the practitioner. **As long as you practice design, you are bound by no limitations to redefining it.**

Principle of No Truth

Truth begins with the expression of the creator. All established processes, patterns, trends, and methodologies begin with an individual's expression of the truth they perceive. **This means that what we follow is simply another person's truth**. If we follow a design pattern, we follow the expression of a practitioner who established the pattern. If we follow a trend, we follow the expression of a practitioner who decided to exceed the limitations of established patterns.

The truth exists because we exist; and no matter how objective it may seem, it is never completely objective.

When we design, it is common for us to follow the processes we have been taught, and to design according to conventions, trends, and best practices. While there is nothing wrong with this approach, crystallization begins when designers continue to practice and pass down to others what they believe or observe to be the "right" way just because it is the established way.

What they believe is the "right" way is simply another person's way.

In fact, there is no right way.

Tradition is an illusion. Truth is relative and never fixed. It is not something that, once established, cannot be changed. What is wrong may be right. What is right may be wrong.

When you acquire this liberty of understanding, it means that you may ultimately express what is your truth even if it defies tradition. **It cannot be invalid because it is, simply, "your way"**.

Those who practice according to the classical pattern understand only its shadows, but not themselves. When you begin to see that truth follows no path, you learn that it is something you must ultimately establish for yourself. You can only do this when you learn to understand yourself, and create an expression true to yourself.

Use motion to evolve. Approach from new angles.

Dynamism

To be dynamic means to be in perpetual motion, changing, adapting, never staying still. It means to be advancing and constantly evolving.

The art of design changes every day, so you must evolve with it. When an art ceases to evolve, it is no longer living. When you cease to evolve, you are no longer alive.

Apply motion to principles. Create intersections between one art and another, one principle and another.

Adopt a beginner's mindset so that you will always be learning. The designer who is dynamic adapts to everyday change, while a static designer ceases to improve and becomes displaced by the advances of everyday change.

Immerse yourself in the change around you, by absorbing everything you come into contact with.

Have an awareness of new trends, unconventional methods, emerging technology, the existence of design in multiple aspects, art, life itself, and all the experiences you come into contact with daily. This will broaden your mindset and perspective, and return to you in a new form of influence when you practice design.

If you practice another form of art, or a hobby, seek to understand its principles deeply. When you reach a profound level of understanding in another form of art, one that you passionately enjoy, you possess the potential to draw from that source into your practice as a designer. You will then understand design in a new light, and with a new way of thinking, all rooted and exemplified from a unique perspective that will set you apart from everyone else. Any form of knowledge that is higher and deeper than design has the potential to cultivate design thinking up to the limits of that knowledge, even if it seems unrelated to design.

You will find that the deepest things you learn about design may not be from design itself. Inspiration comes from the strangest places. The breakthrough moments of great discoveries may actually come from another source, one that you least expect.

We are the sum of all things we experience.

The things we do, and the things we create, come from our expression, externalized into a unique, real-world footprint. We are the seed, so if we nurture ourselves with experiences, a deep understanding of another art, or philosophy, we enrich all externalizations of ourselves.

Your style of design must evolve. If you have designed something, whether it be a button, a website, or an experience, more than a couple of times, consider a new and exploratory way of doing it. Begin with a solid foundation of reasoning for the divergence. Even unconventional approaches can have excellent outcomes as long as the evolution does not cause a negative impact on the experience. Unconventional approaches are absolutely necessary to introduce a new form, a new way of thinking, to the world.

When you enrich yourself, you enrich all externalizations of yourself.

Circle with no circumference
Boundary with no boundaries

Note that this is by no means a complete list of fields that may intersect with interface design. It is not bound to a certain form.

There are constant misconceptions about what is UI and what is UX.

I hope this makes it clear:

If you are an interface designer, you are also a user experience designer. If you are a user experience designer, you are not necessarily an interface designer. The two, however, should never be apart.

There are debates on what user interface is as opposed to experience design, and what an interaction designer does as opposed to a user interface designer. In the ideal world, a user interface designer only deals with visual design, colors, layouts, and typography. In the real world, however, UI / UX Designer duties inevitably vary from company to company. There are times when a company requires user interface designers to code, and sometimes user interface designers may be required to do user testing too.

The ideal definition is a limitation, and trying too hard to draw distinct lines between the different fields will limit your skill set and thinking. **It is much better to accept, and understand the intersections as spectra without definite boundaries.**

While there are certain differences, there are no distinct lines.

As a practitioner of UI / UX, it helps to understand that UI / UX is a circle with no circumference, and that it has a boundary with no boundaries. The more able you are, the more successful you will be.

UI / UX, like many other fields, intersects with other fields. If you design without understanding basic copywriting, your design will be limited. If you understand interaction design, have the capability to produce illustrations, you will be able to come up with greater, more thorough solutions. If you understand the fundamentals of code, you narrow the gap between design and development. If you understand strategy, product design, and product management, you will understand experience beyond the interface, and product execution. And when you practice interface design, your execution will rise beyond those who are too busy trying to debate the definitions.

Do not be just a static designer. It is not enough.

Be a designer in motion.

It is useless to define the boundaries. Advance through them instead.

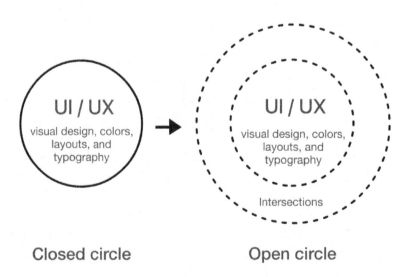

Shift your thinking. Instead of seeing UI / UX as a closed circle, open the circle and and accept the intersections as part of UI / UX design. You will exceed limitations.

Be a dynamic, evolving, designer in motion

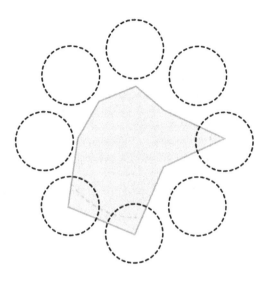

Do not be a static designer

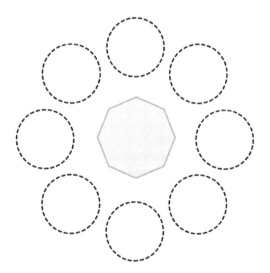

Static vs Dynamic Designer

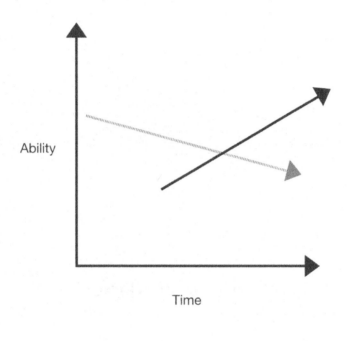

Ability

Time

Static Designer   **Dynamic Designer**

Trajectory and motion are far more important
than a single measurement in time.

60

Even the most "experienced" designers, and the "experts" with ten or more years practicing a single branch of "web design" or "graphic design" hold little relevance to the needs of today if they do not evolve. Time allows for evolution of being, but only if you are in motion with it. If you are not in motion, you limit yourself to only one style, and one branch of understanding.

Length of time and repetition in stale territory do not lead to growth, or new knowledge. Thus it is important to practice being dynamic every couple of repetitions, in order to stay in motion and flow towards greater insights. Innovation has never been the product of convention. Growth only happens in unfamiliar territory.

While we can appreciate skeuomorphism for bridging the gap between humans and technology, it is no longer necessary for the majority of the users today. In 2011, the release of Microsoft's Modern UI for Windows 8 established a particularly influential new form of design that would eventually push digital design into new territory. It set a new standard of interface design specifically made for the digital paradigm.

Technology evolves. Styles evolve, so you must evolve with it. A less experienced designer, but one who understands the modern and timeless concept of how to practice design, holds much greater potential to evolve quickly beyond an experienced but dated one. It is like the less experienced but modern designer compared to the experienced designer who still practices design with shadows and gradients.

As a designer in motion, you position yourself to be ready for new challenges and advance swiftly beyond those who are static. Focus on being in motion, staying in motion, and setting a trajectory.

Dynamism with Formlessness and Expression

Experience and absorb the world in as many ways as you can, but strive for depth, to understand the deepest principles of other arts or disciplines. In this depth you will find new approaches for your own practice.

When you cultivate yourself with higher forms of knowledge, you will absorb new forms of expression, ones which eventually become *your* expression, and will give your practice its brilliance. The knowledge you obtain, and the work you produce, draw on experiences and wisdom that cannot be found inside the field of design itself. If designers were only designers, nothing more, there would be no flavour, no uniqueness, which would result in a very linear, non-diverse, and mundane set of procedures. **Design evolves through expression. Design is dynamic because we are dynamic.**

Knowledge and tradition only represents a single point in time. Forms provide structure but become a limitation if the structure is too rigid to evolve. Dynamic designers are in motion toward achieving better selves by avoiding crystallization of form, and do so by developing an expression true to themselves.

Apply motion to principles.

Apply principles to principles.

Be in motion.

Simplicity and Directness

To understand simplicity is to understand directness, which is a straight line to the objective. It is to deliver a solution without ornamentation. Simplicity stresses efficiency. It aims for minimum work and maximum results, and to find the most efficient solution. It often provides a single answer to multiple problems, one expression that fulfills multiple demands. It accomplishes as much as possible while being as little as possible. It is in constant motion to eliminate the unnecessary.

Simplicity is to reduce, not add.

Directness is a form of simplicity, which follows a straight line to the objective.

To be direct and simple is to be without ornamentation.

To be simple is to continuously shed all inessentials.

Efficiency is to do as much as possible, with as little as possible,

If you must add, add; and then reduce. Always end in reduction.

What is simple can always be simpler.

Simplicity is a constant motion favouring reduction.

Simplicity in UX Design

Simplicity is the greatest contributor to the success of many things. It is the goal of many products. Designers constantly strive for it, but to achieve it, we have to understand it and be able to measure it.

Measure simplicity by the sum of all interactions:

The more interface elements there are, the more time it takes the user to understand it.

The more interactions the user experiences, the longer it takes to reach the goal.

The longer it takes to reach the goal, the more frustration the user feels.

Thus, to achieve simplicity, aim for an interface with as little interface as possible, to require as little interaction as possible, which results in as little experience as possible.

Most designers talk about making a "greater" or "pleasant" user experience. But "greater" and "pleasant" need to be defined. Without a definition, the term is without substance, and without substance it is aimless. A greater experience is not always about enriching or enhancing the experience by adding; rather, at the highest level, it is about enriching, and enhancing the experience by eliminating them, or reducing them until only the essentials are left. Many designers are too caught up with making "pleasant" experiences, through visual and functional appeal. Others are debating form and function, while leaving the truth behind.

It is clear that all designers strive for simplicity; but to achieve it, we have to understand what it means. Simplicity is a movement toward a greater user experience through reduction, not addition. Simplicity can be applied to the design, interface, interaction, and experience as well.

Golden Krishna's *The Best Interface is No Interface* makes a brilliant argument with a very relevant example. In this day and age, our obsession with apps and interfaces has created an app hype, fueling our desire to make an app for everything, even the most trivial tasks, as if this were an advancement. There's an app for almost everything you can think of, including one to unlock your BMW vehicle.

My BMW ConnectedDrive lets BMW owners to lock and unlock their vehicles with their mobile app. Is this really a better user experience? Let's take a look at what it takes to unlock a car door with this app.

The driver approaches the vehicle and takes out the phone.

BMW Remote App

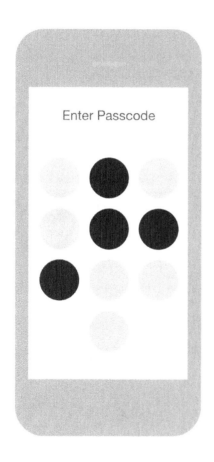

Unlock phone

Navigate and Launch BMW
Connected App

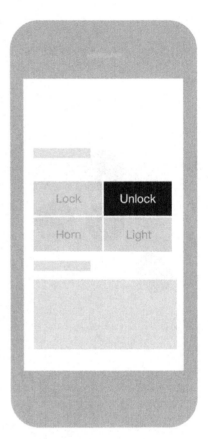

Tap on your vehicle icon

Press and hold "Unlock"

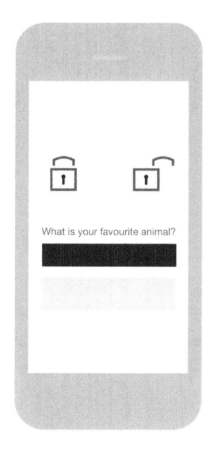

What is your favourite animal?

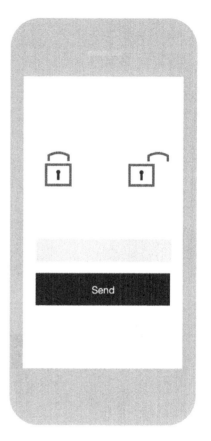

Send

Answer security question   Hit send

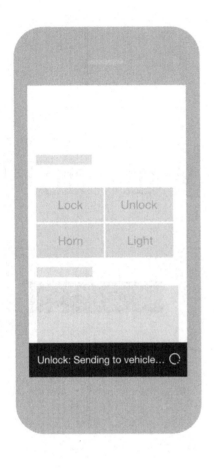

Unlock: Sending to vehicle...

Wait

Wait

Unlock: performed successfully

It takes a minimum of nine steps to simply unlock the car. And that assumes that you entered the phone password correctly, no previous apps were running, and that there is a smooth WiFi and data connection. This also doesn't include account creation and setup. Sending and receiving the unlock signal can take five seconds or more.

The sum of steps performed from beginning to end is the experience. Is this really a better experience, or advancement compared to the conventional key fob? Unlocking a car door shouldn't take more than ten seconds. It should only take an instant. Using a mobile app to perform such a trivial task is unnecessary. The key fob, in comparison, is much more efficient in completing the task.

Experience of Unlocking Your Vehicle

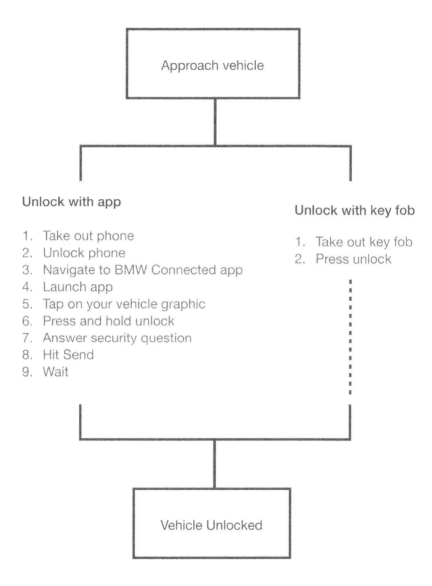

Approach vehicle

Unlock with app

1. Take out phone
2. Unlock phone
3. Navigate to BMW Connected app
4. Launch app
5. Tap on your vehicle graphic
6. Press and hold unlock
7. Answer security question
8. Hit Send
9. Wait

Unlock with key fob

1. Take out key fob
2. Press unlock

Vehicle Unlocked

How can we make unlocking a car easier?

How can we make unlocking a car a better experience?

How do we make it the best experience?

By applying the principles of Simplicity and Directness, we can enhance the experience through reduction. This means eliminating the unnecessary. The key fob, though dated, is still a much better solution than the mobile app because it takes less effort to use. It fact, it takes more work, more time, and more hassle to unlock your vehicle with the app than with the keys.

But compared to the key fob, how can we then make a better experience for unlocking the vehicle?

We can apply the principle of directness, which means following a straight path to the objective, without digression or ornamentation.

Simplicity and Directness

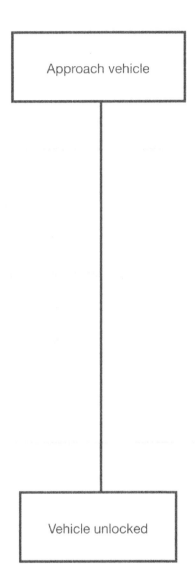

Approach vehicle

Vehicle unlocked

If we follow this approach, all the driver has to do is approach the car, and it will unlock automatically. In fact, Siemens introduced the *SmartKey* technology as early as 1995. The vehicle has low frequency transmitting antennas internally and externally, which can transmit signals to the key. When the key is sufficiently close, the signals activate it and the key transmits a signal back to the vehicle, which then unlocks. Taking out the key is unnecessary. It also has failsafe protocols: it would not allow you to lock your keys inside the vehicle. If you accidentally placed the keys in the trunk, it would not allow you to close your trunk. You cannot lock your keys inside your car. Many car manufacturers are using this technology today.

If we understand the problem objectively, that we are designing a better key for the car to provide a better experience, we see that the experience does not necessarily need to be funneled down to a mobile app solution. If we automatically think "we need an app to unlock the vehicle", we have already missed half our understanding of the problem. This sends our approach off in a mistaken direction, and crystallizes our thinking that we must solve the problem with a mobile app.

It doesn't matter how "playful" or "delightful" the experience of the mobile app is. Even if the interface was beautifully designed by the best designers in the world, the direction and approach at the high level already expose a big limitation. Taking out the phone, unlocking it, and launching an app already takes more steps than taking out a key fob and pushing "unlock".

The *SmartKey* technology solves the problem without the user interface of the mobile app. It also eliminates the need to push buttons on a conventional key fob to unlock the vehicle. It has eliminated the need of a user interface. So while Golden Krishna asserts that the best interface is no interface, we could go further:

Where there is no user interface, there is no interaction, and where there is no interaction, there is no experience.

This brings me to my next point.

The Best Experience is No Experience

[handwritten: Or is it one, know the user doesn't they are living.]

As technology gets better, it does more for the human user. It takes our tasks and our human effort away, and can make processes more efficient. It takes time to comprehend, and act through, even the simplest interface. The more interactions and interfaces there are, the more time it takes to do what you want to do. But as the designs get better, human effort seems to transfer from the human to the computer, requiring less of an interface and less interaction. Ultimately, this progression should result in achieving a design that requires no human effort, no interface and thus no interaction. Where there is no interaction, there is no experience.

This is not to say that the design does not exist. Rather it exists at a high level of complexity and low level of visibility, transferring all effort from humans to technology.

SmartKey technology is a great example. Instead of requiring us to push a button to unlock the vehicle, it does that for us. It does the work for us, so our experience of unlocking the vehicle no longer exists. It enhances our overall experience with the car by eliminating part of that experience.

In the simplest terms, the spectrum of user experience ranges from bad to good. But far beyond good is not great nor excellent: it is simply non-existent.

The Spectrum of Experience

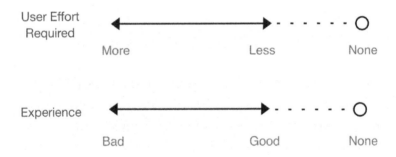

Perfection is an interface without an interface, an interaction without an interaction, which *lets users achieve goals without achieving goals.* This is called *the experienceless experience; to have an experience without an experience.* You experience unlocking n without actually unlocking it.

How can we apply the implications of this philosophy to, say, the experience of driving? How can we design a better user interface for the dashboard?

We can eliminate the experience of driving. We can also eliminate the dashboard.

For decades, car manufacturers' perspective towards car production has emphasized improving the driving experience, focusing on streamlining user interactions and improving the overall sense of ease a user has when operating one of their models. In many television ads, most of the information focuses on updated and modernized accessibility, ease of maintenance, and the overall positive experience of the vehicle.

The selling points that we see are universal and recurrent: sleek and modernized dashboards, easier accessibility with radio and Bluetooth, two-wheel, four-wheel drive options, improved camera and backup assistance. The bedrock for most manufacturers' pitches is asserting that the *physical operation* of a vehicle is comfortable and practicable.

On the other hand, Tesla Motors, an American automaker specializing in electric cars and self-driving vehicles, had a rather brilliant approach: Tesla seems to have decided to circumvent this common practice of selling users on the *physical* operation of a vehicle by shifting the focus of their development and advertisement to the *self-driving* vehicle. Rather than giving the experience of driving, Tesla instead promotes the choice of eliminating it.

When we eliminate the experience of driving, we are completely liberated, and gain the freedom to choose what we actually want to experience. We can sleep instead of drive. Eat instead of drive. If we desire, we may even choose to drive.

We can sum this up as a principle of direction:

No interface as interface.

No interaction as interaction

No experience as experience.

So we can achieve goals without achieving goals

To have no experience is to have every experience.

To examine the experience of unlocking a vehicle at a higher level, we examine the experience of driving. We can apply the philosophy of *no experience* at low or high levels. As we apply it to designing a better experience for the everyday flow of daily living, clear truths will reveal themselves.

We can already eliminate the driving experience with self-driving vehicles. We may even go as far as complete vehicle autonomy.

Experience of conventional driving

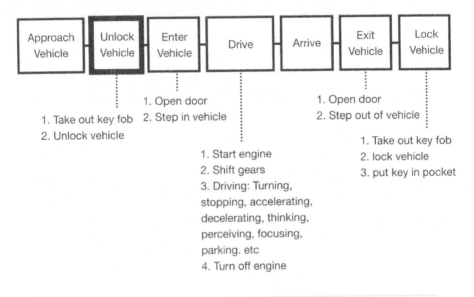

1. Take out key fob
2. Unlock vehicle

1. Open door
2. Step in vehicle

1. Start engine
2. Shift gears
3. Driving: Turning, stopping, accelerating, decelerating, thinking, perceiving, focusing, parking. etc
4. Turn off engine

1. Open door
2. Step out of vehicle

1. Take out key fob
2. lock vehicle
3. put key in pocket

Experience of self-driving, autonomous vehicle

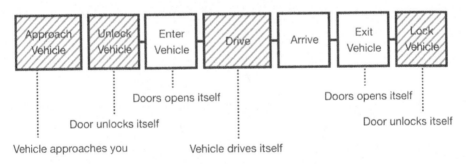

Doors opens itself

Door unlocks itself

Vehicle approaches you

Vehicle drives itself

Doors opens itself

Door unlocks itself

Result - Experience of driverless driving

Complete autonomy not only includes the elimination of driving via self-driving, but eliminates the driving experience from end to end. Instead of you approaching the vehicle, the vehicle approaches you. Instead of unlocking the vehicle and opening the door, the vehicle does it for you. All you have to do is enter and exit the vehicle.

What we currently understand and accept as "driving" is a fixed form. Because forms will ultimately be subject to limitations, "driving" will eventually dissolve and rise again with a new meaning and a new form.

How can we design a better shopping experience?

We can do our best to eliminate it.

Conventional Shopping

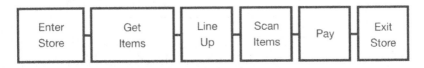

Amazon Go

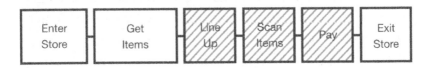

Result

Amazon Go is a new kind of store which features the world's most advanced shopping technology by eliminating lines and checkout. With cutting-edge computer vision, sensor fusion, and deep learning that automatically tracks items from the shelf to the cart, all the user simply has to do is grab and go. This goes a long way toward eliminating the shopping experience. This precursor will eventually lead to shopping without shopping.

How can we design a better login?

We can certainly improve a simple login interface by providing flexibility around logging in, such as letting the user provide a registered email address instead of a user name or letting the user know that they've attempted to log in with a user name that doesn't exist. We can also remind them that they've entered an old password that they changed a month ago, to help prompt their memory. In addition we can offer social-network logins with Google or Facebook credentials for a quicker entry.

However, working within a form will ultimately become a limitation. To exceed such a limitation, we must introduce a new form to the world. If we examine this at a higher level, and apply the principle of no experience, it is apparent that the best login experience is to have logged in without logging in. That's why Google's Project Abacus plans to kill passwords. Project Abacus introduces authentication that calculates a "Trust Score" based on factors such as facial recognition and your typing and voice patterns. The goal is to eliminate the hassle of remembering and typing in passwords and user names.

The best experience is no experience, and no experience is the best experience.

It is to have driven without driving.

To have shopped without shopping.

To have logged in without logging in.

It is a principle of action without action

If we cannot reach the level of no experience, we can assume dynamism, and formlessness to conceive a more plausible outcome.

To have no experience is to have every experience.

When we apply directness to design, we see a clear and straight line to the objective, without ornamentation. Simplicity reveals itself through directness. Directness can be formless. We can apply it at a low level or a high level. We can apply experienceless experience to all flows. When you understand design in totality, you understand that a solution does not necessarily need to manifest itself in a mobile app, or with dashing user interfaces. When you understand that the best experience is ultimately no experience, you simply understand that there is nothing easier than doing nothing at all.

Forms are a trap. Crystallization prevents fluidity, but formlessness is capable of assuming all forms. Ultimately, the best experience is no experience, and to have no experience is to have every experience. It is perfection. But note that while perfection is not always attainable, it always exists for us to strive towards. It provides a trajectory so that we may have a direction to improve our designs.

If you cannot reach perfection, then you can assume formlessness which allows "best" or "greater" experiences to be redefined to what is attainable. While the definition of "best experience" is to have no experience, remember that definitions are not bound to a fixed form. However, perfection must exist in some form of the definition of experience, so that it may be a guiding principle for all designers to understand and strive for.

Design Principles

Obey these principles without being bound to them.

1

Great experiences are not enough.
Strive to eliminate them.

2

Perfection is to shed everything until only the essentials are left.

3

Continuously enhance a design through reduction. If you must add, add, and then reduce; but always end in reduction.

4

Seek the truth, even if it defies tradition, and even if it follows tradition.

5

There are no limitations to design, as long as it does not violate the fundamentals.

6

Use what works, as long as it works.
Do not be too concerned with styles.

7

Truth is living, therefore changing.

Principles of Being

Water Principle

Water is devoid of form, thus unlimited in form. It is abstract. It is concrete, but never fully solid. It is tense, yet relaxed. It is the essence of fluidity which allows for endless expansion, and ability to shift between forms. It is clear and free from judgment. It has no ego. What is, is.

Be like water.

When one form does not work, be fluid, then concrete again.

Use the essence of abstraction to draw a new understanding into a new form.

Water can have form. It also has fluidity to be formless in an instant.

Water can find the smallest weakness in the strongest walls.

Temporary blocks do not stop its flow.

The knowledge that you possess is concrete. In order to expand it, your knowledge must dissolve into abstraction, so that in this abstraction new knowledge can emerge in a new form. As a human being, do not be fixed on doing things a certain way, or commit to thinking a certain way. You must be clear, and be able to shift your mentality fluidly, so you can conquer obstacles by finding a way around them.

Design · Test
Form – Formless
Concrete · Abstract
Knowledge – – – – – – – – – – – – – – – – – – – Greater Knowledge
Limitation · New Limitation
Expression – – – – – – – – – – – – – – – – – – Feedback

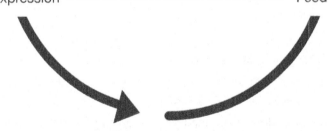

Principle of Circular Motion

The principle of circular motion is a principle of motion for growth. Use it as a mirror to discover yourself. Each iteration is an improved understanding of self, methods, knowledge, expression and more. To improve all expressions of oneself is to see the self in relation with another.

This principle can first and foremost be used to test designs. Every cycle and iteration improves not only the design, but also one's self-knowledge.

When you reach the limits of a form, the form becomes a limitation. In order to exceed it, you must break down the current form so a new form can emerge. Without willingness to adapt, to accept the nature of change, there can be no growth.

Old knowledge can be dissolved so that new knowledge may take its place. When you exceed your limitations, your new limitation becomes your current one. When you express yourself in relation to another, you gain wisdom which allows your expression to evolve.

Use the principle of circular motion to subdue a greater force by redirection. One of the greatest qualities a designer may possess is the ability to face criticism without opposition, and to utilize it to forge a better self. The designer does not withdraw in the presence of greater competition, but rather utilizes it for all avenues of growth.

Principle of Non-Resistance

The principle of non-resistance is the principal balance of nature, and a combination of the water principle and the principle of circular motion.

Force met with force will only cause destruction. But when force is met without force, it can be grasped and redirected for a better purpose. We don't always possess the greater force, so we must yield to it, but find a way around it.

Opposition to new ideas, new methods, and new ways will only prevent enlightenment.

Resistance will only lead to crystallization of what was once fluid.

Draw from those with greater experience than yourself, and take what you gain as an opportunity for growth instead of perceiving it as competition.

Forms are meant to be broken. New forms emerge when old forms are broken. Non-resistance welcomes change by simply flowing.

Conclusion

The Tao of Design and User Experience is a set of guiding principles and philosophies meant to liberate you as the practitioner of design. It is not meant to teach you a specific way to design specific things; rather, it begins with the solidification of knowledge of self and of the fundamentals of design in order to create a strong foundation and a proper trajectory. With these principles, and a proper trajectory, you may foster unlimited ways of knowing, especially in the unknown, and create a way when there is no way. All designers, no matter how experienced, should never forget the basics of design, as all branches of knowledge and externalization stem from the root.

These principles can open your mind to abstraction, and introduce to you the highest level of thinking so you may reach out to a boundless boundary to draw new understandings, and create a new form.

Remember that knowledge only represents a point in time, so our knowledge on design only represents a point in time. When knowledge becomes bound to a certain form, that knowledge will ultimately become a limitation. So rather than introducing knowledge, it is much more crucial to introduce abstraction and a set of guiding principles which cultivates a way of thinking so that you are capable of forming new knowledge.

The principles themselves are not bound to a specific form, so they are capable of providing a direction for growth beyond the field of design. Put the principles and philosophies to practice daily, and use them as a mirror to discover yourself and understand yourself. When you understand yourself, you will be able to foster your own set of principles and approaches. A strong foundation yields action with meaningful intent, which, in design, will naturally demonstrate itself by revealing well thought out and well rationalized solutions.

Understanding of self and fostering a way of knowing will allow you to be clear. Clarity will enable you to dissolve obstructions that prevent you from seeing the real truth. When you simply understand yourself, you are able to see the truth clearly.

Practice formlessness in all aspects. Be dynamic, and apply motion to yourself so that you may evolve. Understand and develop your own way of expression so you are able to remove yourself from limitations, and introduce new forms to the world. Use simplicity and directness to guide you to the truth without obstructions.

When it comes to designing for experience, no experience is ultimately the best experience. When you are able to see the light in this and fully absorb and apply the principles here, you will begin to master yourself, and master the art of design and user experience.

Selected inspirational quotes from Bruce Lee

A note from the author

Design is a form of art. Martial arts is also a form of art. These are just some of the wisdom which has guided me in writing this book.

me of these quotations are from *The Tao of Jeet Kune Do*. Some can be found circulating on the internet.

Adapt what is useful, reject what is useless, and add what is specifically your own.

All fixed set patterns are incapable of adaptability or pliability.

The truth is outside of all fixed patterns.

Running water never grows stale.

Art is an expression of life and transcends both time and space. We must employ our own souls through art to give a new form and a new meaning to nature or the world

The classical man is just a bundle of routine, ideas and tradition. When he acts, he is translating every living movement in terms of the old.

If any style teaches you a method of fighting, then you might be able to fight according to the limits of that method, but that is not actually fighting.

If you follow the classical pattern, you are understanding the routine, the tradition, the shadow – you are not understanding yourself.

Observe what is with undivided awareness.

About The Author

Andrew Ou is a formless and dynamic designer, author, and UI/UX expert capable of taking ideas to launch. Outside his career, he loves movies, pizza, board games, video games, and, of course, martial arts. He holds a Bachelor of Science from The School of Interactive Arts and Technology at Simon Fraser University.

Through his speaking engagement and consulting services, he helps accelerate designers and companies by removing them from limitations so they can see the truth, and discover a clear way.

If this book has helped liberate you in any way, please consider leaving a 5 star rating on Amazon.com

Got questions or don't understand something?
Email him at **andrew.ou@outlook.com**

Get more from Andrew

Additional articles on Medium.com

Follow him on Medium.com
https://medium.com/@andrewou99

You don't always need to follow native Android or iOS patterns when designing an app (Formlessness)
http://bit.ly/2VGj9Mn

The art in design you cannot ignore (Expression)
bit.ly/2lIP7Yx

Get exclusive UX design training and mentorship from Andrew

- Additional training videos with practical applications
- Get 1-on-1 Design Mentorship
- Invite Andrew to train your in-house design team
- Invite Andrew to speak at your event

Learn more at Taodesignux.com

Made in the USA
Coppell, TX
01 May 2020